Getting To Know
Your Kitten

Getting To Know Your Kitten

Gill Page

INTERPET PUBLISHING

The Author

Gill Page has been involved with a wide variety of animals for many years. She has run a successful pet centre and for some time helped in rescuing and re-homing unwanted animals. She has cared for many animals of her own and is keen to pass on her experience so that children may learn how to look after their pets lovingly and responsibly.

Published by Interpet Publishing,
Vincent Lane,
Dorking,
Surrey RH4 3YX,
England

© 2000 Interpet Publishing Ltd.
All rights reserved

ISBN 1-84286-109-3

The recommendations in this book are given without any guarantees on the part of the author and publisher. If in doubt, seek the advice of a vet or pet-care specialist.

Credits

Editor: Philip de Ste. Croix

Designer: Phil Clucas MSIAD

Studio photography: Neil Sutherland

Colour artwork: Rod Ferring

Production management: Consortium, Poslingford, Suffolk CO10 8RA

Print production: SNP Leefung, China

Printed and bound in the Far East

Contents

Making Friends   6

Getting To Know Me   8

Taking Me Home   10

My First Day At Home   12

Toilet Training   14

Time For Bed   16

My Favourite Foods   18

Meal Times   20

Treats and Titbits   22

Playtime   24

Safe Play   26

Looking My Best   28

My Own Front Door   30

Keeping Fit and Well   32

Health Check   34

Girl or Boy?   36

What If I Do Have Kittens?   38

My Special Page   40

Kitten Check List   41

My Relations   42

A Note To Parents   46

Acknowledgements   48

Making Friends

Hello. I am your new friend. What is your name? I will need a name too. I am quite clever, so I will soon learn to come when you call me. I will tell you a few things about myself and then you will know how to take care of me. I love playing with toys and we could do that together – you could make some toys for me, a long piece of string that looks like a wiggly worm is good. As I am only young I will get tired easily; when I am looking sleepy will you pop me into my bed so that I can have a snooze? Do you have a soft bed? I would like one too.

When we are friends we can play all sorts of games together, but don't make me too tired.

Cats have been living with people for more than 4,000 years.

My mother has shown me how to keep my fur clean by licking it, but you could help by gently brushing me. I like being stroked and I will show you how happy I am by purring. I will become very hungry when I am playing, so when you have your meals please can you make sure I have mine too? I will always need a bowl of fresh water to drink when I am thirsty.

Kittens clean their fur by licking it.

Getting To Know Me

I have a nice multi-coloured coat, but there are lots of other colours to choose from. I will tell you about some of them. There are orange cats – you would call them ginger – and black and grey ones, called tabby. Black cats may have white paws. White cats that have blue eyes often cannot hear very well. Cats that have lots of different colours in their coats are called tortoiseshell and they are nearly always girls. Boy cats are called toms and girl cats are called queens. Some of us have long, fluffy hair, but kittens with short hair are easier to care for.

It will be hard to tell what I will look like when I grow up. I might be a big, fat cat or I could be a small, sleek one. Some kittens grow very tall, but I will only get to be about 30cm (12in) high. I must tell you how I like to be picked up. I need to feel safe and to know that you will not drop me. Gently hold me with one hand under my front feet and the other under my back feet and my bottom.

I like to feel safe when you pick me up and hold me in your arms. Please make sure that you support me well with one hand securely under my back legs and bottom. The other one can support the front part of my body.

~ 9

Taking Me Home

You can choose me in a pet shop, from a family home, or a rescue centre which is a place where stray cats and their kittens are often looked after. I should be playful and have bright, shiny eyes. If I am sitting very quietly in a corner and I do not want to play, it may be because I am not very well. Ask how old I am. I should be eight weeks old before I am taken to my new home. If I am going to be left on my own a lot, I would like to take a brother or sister with me; then we will have each other to play with while you are out.

When I was born I was tiny – I only weighed around 90 grams (3oz), about the same as a small bar of chocolate.

You will need a carrying basket to take me home. Some are made of cardboard, but they may be dark inside and this could frighten me. I like to see where I am going, so please can I have a basket with a wire front to it? To make it cosy put a blanket in the bottom. If we are going home in a car, put me in a safe place where the basket can't fall over. If we will be driving for a long time I would like some water to drink on the way. Most kittens are like me – a moggy (this means I am a mix of breeds) or you may buy a purebred kitten.

My First Day
At Home

I am happy that I will be living with you, but I will be
scared on my first day in your house. I may try to hide.
A good place is up the chimney, so if you have one at
home, ask mummy or daddy to put something in front
of it. Keep me in one room that has been made safe,
with no places where I might get stuck. Do you have
any other pet friends living with you? If you do, please
stay with me when I first meet them. Dogs might chase
me and other cats could be very horrid and hiss at me,
and may even scratch me. We will all soon be friends,
but until we are, leave me in a room on my own
when you are out or have gone to bed.

I may try to scratch or chew things in your house.

I am very nosy and can get into all sorts of trouble.
One of the best games is to climb up the curtains,
but I do look a bit silly when
I cannot get back down. That is
when you will have to help me.
Tidy away your toys or I may
take them to play with myself.
With lots of love from you,
I know I will be fine.

Toilet Training

This might not be a very nice thing to talk about, but even you had to be house-trained when you were little. Kittens do not wear nappies; they have to use a litter tray. While I am young I will have to be kept indoors, so I will need something to use as a toilet. A litter tray is a tray or box that does not leak. There are lots of nice plastic ones to choose from that are easy for you to keep clean. You will have to fill it with cat litter or earth for me to sit in.

When I am properly house-trained, I can be left to play happily indoors for hours.

As soon as you bring me home, put me on my litter tray
so that I know where it is. If you do this every time I
have something to eat or drink, or when I wake up, I will
soon learn what it is for. You can even buy me a litter
tray that has a hood or cover on it. Then I cannot make
a mess by scratching up all the litter and scattering it all
over the floor. The tray will have to be cleaned out every
day, but if you are a little person it's probably better if
a grown-up does this job for you.

Time For Bed

I like to spend a lot of my time asleep. Is your bed soft and warm? I will want a bed like that too or I might try and share your bed. I want my bed to be where I can be left alone to rest and where people's feet cannot trample on me. There are some really smart beds that you can buy from the pet shop, but I will be just as happy with a large cardboard box.

To keep me safe when I first come to live with you, put
my bed into a large, wire cage. I can be shut in at night.
Put my litter tray in with me and some water for me to
drink and then I will have all that I need. When I am used
to living with you, I will not need to be shut in at night.

Put a blanket in the bottom of my bed. You have
blankets or duvets which cover you to keep you warm,
but I just sit on mine. Please do not tuck me in or cover
me up. It will be hard for me to get out and it could
even stop me breathing.

In cold weather
I may cover my face
with my tail to keep
it warm.

My Favourite Foods

When I am little I will need four small meals every day, but by the time I am one year old, I will only need two. You can find out how much food to give me on page 21. Before you bring me home, find out what I have been eating. If you give me the same sort of food to start with, I will not have an upset tummy. After a while you can try me with all sorts of food to see which I like the best. If I have lots of different sorts of food to try when I am young, I will not be fussy about what I eat when I grow up.

You can give me cooked fish or chicken to eat. I also like tinned or dried food. I must have a bowl of fresh water too. A saucer of milk is yummy, but one a day is enough – if I am greedy and drink too much of it I will have a bad tummy ache. I must not eat bones. They might get stuck in my throat. If I have fish to eat, please take any bones out for me. I hate food that is very cold. Food that is cold makes my teeth feel funny. Does cold food do that to your teeth?

Milk is nice, but too much will give me a tummy ache.

Meal Times

I will need two dishes, one for my food and another for my water. You could buy dishes that have my name painted on them. I will know that they are mine, but it won't stop me from taking food from other pet dishes. So that I don't get into trouble, you should stand and watch me when I am eating and stop me from taking food from my friends.

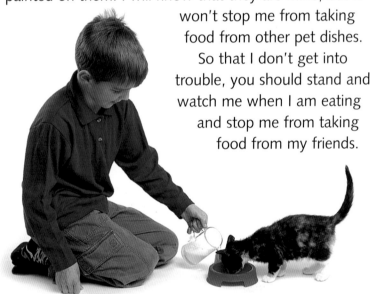

Dishes that are heavy cannot be pushed around the floor when I am eating. People may get cross if I tip my dish up and the food is spilt. I like my dishes to be kept very clean; please wash them every day. You will see when I don't like the smell of something – I will walk away and shake my paws at you. We should not share plates, even though I often think the food on your plate is nicer than my own.

Feeding Timetable

I have a small tummy and only need small meals. An ordinary teaspoon can be used to measure out my food.

- **8–12 weeks old:** Four meals a day – breakfast, lunch, supper, dinner – last thing at night. Three spoonfuls at each meal.

  Two meals of meat and two of cereal and milk. The cereal has to be a cooked one. An easy-to-cook porridge is something I love, but it has to cool down before you give it to me.

- **12–18 weeks:** Three meals a day – breakfast, lunch, supper. Six to eight spoonfuls at each meal.
  Two meals of meat and one of cereal and milk.

- **18–26 weeks:** Three meals a day as before, but nine to 12 spoonfuls at each meal.

- **26 weeks and older:** Two meals a day – breakfast and supper.

  Two meals of meat. If I am having tinned cat food, read and follow the instructions on the tin.

Treats and Titbits

I like a few snacks between meals. I expect you do too.
I must not eat your snacks. Salt and chocolate are very
bad for me and they will make me feel ill. You can
buy chocolate drops made just for cats, but they are
my treats – I do not want to see you eating them.
The pet shop has some tasty biscuits that have a
fishy taste – I love those. When I have to use
the cat flap for the first time, you can use
a treat to show me the way through.

I love a bowl like this that has fresh grass in it for me to eat.

A treat I really enjoy, and one I must have if I live indoors all the time, is grass. I need to eat the grass to help my tummy digest food, just as you need to eat green vegetables. It adds fibre to my diet and has vitamins in it. I use it to make myself sick too – so watch out! You can buy a little pot from the pet shop that has grass seed in it. When you get home pour water on it and in a few days grass will grow. It is called kitty or cat grass. Or you could dig up a piece of lawn and put in a small pot. Only use clean grass. I will need fresh grass every week.

Playtime

Toys and playtime
mean a lot to me.
That is when we can
have fun together. I enjoy
playing with my toys as much
as you do. Playing with toys
when I am young helps to
make me fit and strong.
Even when I have grown
up, I will still want to play
games with you. I love to
scratch with my claws. If you buy
me a scratch post I will soon learn to
sharpen my claws on that and not on
the sofa. Mummies and daddies get
very, very cross when I do that.

Some of my cat friends think that woolly jumpers and socks are fun to chew, but if you don't leave them lying around I won't be able to nibble them. Some toys have the leaves of a plant called cat-nip in them. I think it is a lovely smell and I will play for hours with a cat-nip toy. But I am just as happy to play with toys which you have made for me. A cotton reel tied to a long piece of string is good. I can even have a good time playing hide and seek in a cardboard box or under a page of a newspaper.

When I rub against you, I am leaving my scent mark on you.

Safe Play

Playtime is really cool, but please make sure my play area is safe for me. There are lots of things in the house that I will like to chew. Electric wires will kill me if I try to eat them. Even if an iron is not plugged in, I could still pull the heavy iron down on top of me. That will really hurt, so please be careful. Some of the pretty plants that you have in the house could make me ill if I chew them. Even if they did not hurt me I will spoil them, so put the plants in a place where I cannot reach them.

If my whiskers fit through a gap, then I know that the rest of my body will too.

Before mummy turns on the washing machine or dryer look to see if I am hiding inside. As I get bigger, I can play in the garden or yard. I will try and climb trees, but sometimes I cannot find my way down again and a grown-up will have to rescue me. You must not try and help me or we will both be stuck up the tree. I will need to learn how to use a cat flap so that I can dash into the house if something frightens me (see pages 30-31).

Looking My Best

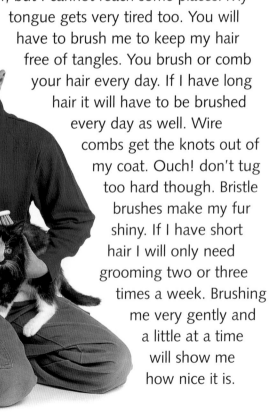

I will need some help to keep my fur looking smart. I can do a lot myself, but I cannot reach some places. My tongue gets very tired too. You will have to brush me to keep my hair free of tangles. You brush or comb your hair every day. If I have long hair it will have to be brushed every day as well. Wire combs get the knots out of my coat. Ouch! don't tug too hard though. Bristle brushes make my fur shiny. If I have short hair I will only need grooming two or three times a week. Brushing me very gently and a little at a time will show me how nice it is.

My tongue is covered with very fine spikes. I use it like a comb on my fur.

When I am little you can sit me on your lap to brush me. If I am too big, stand me on a table that has a towel spread over it to stop me slipping. Start with my back and always brush my hair from my head towards my tail. I change my coat twice a year. This is called moulting. I feel quite itchy at these times. Combing helps and it stops my loose fur from sticking to the furniture and your clothes.

My Own Front Door

Cat flaps are my own little doorway into the house. I can get in and out when I need to. I will have to be shown how to use one. Before I can go out on my own I will have to get used to wearing a collar. In case I get lost put a tag on the collar with my name and address on it. I will hate it when you first put one on. Buy me a stretchy one, so that I can wriggle out of it if I get it stuck on a twig or wire. A collar that glows in the dark makes it easy for car drivers to see me at night.

When I wag my tail it means I am cross, not happy like a dog.

Show me how the cat flap works. Open it and call me through. Offering me one of my favourite treats will make me brave enough to jump through. I will soon learn. I will have to slip through quickly in case my tail gets shut in the door. If other cats try to come in you can buy a special cat flap and collar – called a magnetic one. When I am wearing the special collar that unlocks the flap I will be the only cat that can come in.

Keeping Fit and Well

My doctor is called a vet. He will look after me when I am sick, but he also helps to keep me fit and well. When my mother was feeding me with her milk, I was safe from any diseases. Now that I am living with you I need injections to protect me from cat 'flu and other nasty bugs. The vet will give me my first injections at eight or nine weeks old. I will need another one when I am 12 weeks. I must go back to the vet every year for booster jabs.

If I am tagged with a microchip, it will be easy for a vet to find out to whom I belong. He can read the chip with a scanner, like this.

I am a kitten now, but I can live to be 17 years old, and sometimes even longer.

The vet will check me over for other things too. All cats can have worms. They are special worms that feed and live in my tummy and are very bad for me. The vet has pills that you can give me to kill the worms. He will check my fur for fleas. To stop me becoming a mummy or daddy I can have a special operation. The vet will do this for me when I am about six months old. My vet can also microchip me, so that if I am lost or stolen other vets who may find me will know who my real owner is. Take me to the vet in a cat basket. I will not be able to run away and other animals in the waiting room will not be able to scare me.

Health Check

Here's a list of things to check to make sure I'm healthy and feeling good!

1. Appetite. Am I eating well? See that I am not being sick. Do I eat a lot but am I still very thin? That might mean I need worming.

2. Breathing. I should breathe easily and quietly, no coughing or choking.

3. Body. I should be round and plump. Do I have a nice clean bottom?

4. Claws Not too long or split. No thorns or splinters in my feet.

5. Coat. Clean and shiny. Not too many loose hairs. No bald patches.

6. Behaviour. Am I playful and lively? Alert and attentive, not droopy or tired?

7. Ears. Are they pricked so that I can hear everything, not itchy or smelly?

8. Eyes. They should be clear and bright, not sticky or watering as if I am crying.

9. Mouth and teeth. I should have nice clean teeth and pink gums. No bad breath.

My ears may get dirty inside. Get a grown-up to show you how to clean them gently.

If I do not look very well or have hurt myself
I need to be taken to the vet quickly.

My vet's name

My vet's telephone number

Date of my first injection

Date of my second injection

Dates for my booster injections

Girl or Boy?

It is up to you to decide if you would like to have a girl or a boy kitten as your friend. There are hundreds of cute kittens like me that want a friend like you to live with. A lot of them are not as lucky as I am and never have a happy home. You will keep me safe and feed and care for me. I do not need to have kittens myself when I grow up. My vet will take me into hospital for a day for an operation and I will be neutered. This means that I will not have any babies when I grow up. I will be a bit sleepy when I get home, but after a good rest I will be fine.

I have just had my operation. There is only a little bit of my fur missing. My vet says that the hair will soon grow back.

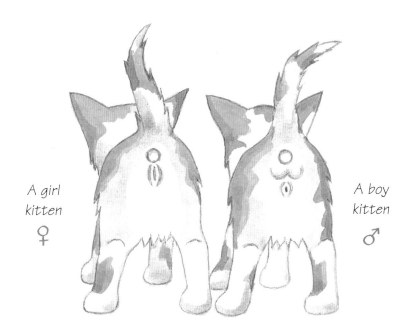

A girl
kitten
♀

A boy
kitten
♂

To tell what sex I am you will have to look under my tail.
Girl kittens have two holes close together. Boy kittens
also have two holes – but they are further apart. Boy cats
that do not have the operation will be rather smelly and
will do a lot of fighting. Girl cats will keep having kittens;
this is bad for them and it is hard to find homes for all
the kittens. A vet will be able to tell you if I am a girl
or boy if you are not sure.

If I have to be
weighed, first weigh yourself
on the bathroom scales, then
do it again holding me. Take
away your weight from this
figure to find mine.

What If I Do Have Kittens?

Just in case I do have kittens, I will tell you what to do. I will need a quiet place to look after my babies and I hope you will not touch them too much at first. Give me a large box where the kittens will be safe, but I can get in and out. I will need extra food so that I can make a lot of milk to feed them.

My mummy carried me in her tummy for 65 days before I was born.

I can have from one to eight babies. They are born with their eyes closed and their ears folded back. They will not be able to see or hear for a while. I will keep them warm, dry, clean and safe. At three weeks old their eyes will be open, their ears will be straight and they will start to play.

Now the kittens will need to be fed with a little bit of meat and some milk. Use milk specially made for kittens or human baby milk (this is a powder and you mix it with the right amount of water). When they are eight weeks old I will not be feeding them any more. They should have four meals a day (see pages 20-21) and will be ready to go to new homes.

My Special Page

My name is

My birthday is

I came from (name of pet
shop or breeder)

Please put a
photograph or a
picture of me
here

Date I came to my new home

My colour is

My fur is

My favourite toy is

My favourite food is

Where I stay when you are on holiday

Kitten Check List

Every day
1 Clean plates and water bowls

2 Feed me and give me fresh water

3 Brush me

4 Check my litter tray, clean it and add extra litter

5 Check for any cuts and scratches

Every week
1 Wash my bedding

2 Wash out my litter tray, dry and refill it

3 Health check – look at the health check list on page 34

4 Look at my toys. Throw away any that are falling apart –
I might choke on small broken bits or swallow them

5 Wash my brush and comb

My Relations

The usual sort of cat that you will probably choose as your friend is a crossbreed or "moggy" like me. We are a mix of breeds, like mongrel puppies. I can be one colour or a mixture. I may not even be the same colour as my brothers and sisters. Here are some of the colours you will be able to choose from. Tabby – a mixture of black and grey fur and my coat will look as though I have stripes or spots. Ginger – a lovely orange colour. I may have creamy golden fur or I might be the colour of marmalade.

Ginger kittens have lovely orange-coloured coats.

A bib

A kitten's
sock

If I am an all-black cat I will look like a mini black panther. A tortoiseshell cat has a mixture of black, brown and orange fur. I may be called a blue cat. I am not really blue but I only have grey hairs in my coat. I may have all-white fur – in that case choose me if I have brown or green eyes. Sadly white cats with no other colour in their fur that have blue eyes are often deaf. I will have short or long hair. I can have white paws, these are called socks. Or a white patch under my chin, called a bib.

My Relations

Instead of a moggy, you might want to buy a purebred kitten, called a pedigree. You will know what I will look like when I am grown up because I will be the same as my mummy and daddy. Each pedigree cat has its own special "posh" name and each breed has certain things about it that make the cat easy to recognize.

There are lots of different breeds. I will tell you about some of them. A Persian has a lot of long fluffy hair in a lot of different colours. They have round faces with a squashed-up nose. Siamese have short creamy coloured hair. Their ears, legs and tails are usually dark brown or blue, but there are other colours too.

I am a Persian kitten with white fluffy fur.

We are Bengal kittens with "leopard" spots.

A Siamese cat is slim with long thin legs. Burmese are like Siamese, but are a little fatter and their fur is a single colour. The Maine Coon is a really large cat – they can be bigger than a small dog. A strange breed is the Rex cat. It has almost no hair at all. Another strange one is called a Turkish Van. These cats love to go swimming. They are white with patches of ginger or cream.

My friends the Manx cats are special – they are born without tails.

A Note To Parents

Having pets is fun and the relationship between a child and a pet can be a magical one. I hope this book will encourage new, young pet owners to look after their pets responsibly and enjoyably. Obviously parents will have to play a supervisory role, not only in daily care, but to explain that the new pet is a living being and not a toy. A well-cared-for pet is a happy one and will reward the whole family with unconditional love. Parents also have to bear the financial costs. Veterinary care can be eased with the help of Pet Health Insurance, well worth the annual premiums. Most veterinary clinics will have leaflets about pet insurance available. Worming and de-fleaing is another chore that parents will need to cope with!

Some of the subjects covered in this book may seem over-simplified to an adult, but I have tried to avoid too much technical detail. Remember that the book is aimed at relatively young children. The subject of giving birth has been touched upon, but the necessity of neutering kittens cannot be stressed too strongly. So many cats and kittens have to be put to sleep because homes cannot be found for them. You may be able to help alleviate this problem by choosing a kitten from one of many rescue centres that cares for unwanted animals.

Acknowledgements

The author and publisher would like to thank the owners who generously allowed their pets to be photographed for this book, and the children who agreed to be models. Specifically they would like to thank Donna and Trevor Strowger and Ellie, Sean and Sam Reeves and Buffy, and Florence Elphick. Thanks also to Stephen Edgington of Hassocks Pet Centre, Denis Blades of Gattleys, Storrington, Steyning Pet Shop, Neil Martin of Washington Garden Centre, Washington, Interpet Limited and Farthings Veterinary Group, Billingshurst.

Thanks are due to the following photographers and picture libraries who kindly supplied photographs that are reproduced in this book.
Geoff du Feu/RSPCA Photolibrary: 26, 42.
Angela Hampton/RSPCA Photolibrary: 2, 13, 32, 38, 39, 44, 46.
Marc Henrie: 45.
E.A. Janes/RSPCA Photolibrary: 27.
Alan Robinson/RSPCA Photolibrary: 43.